# A SEASON IN HELL, THE DRUNKEN BOAT, AND ILLUMINATIONS

## By ARTHUR RIMBAUD

A Season in Hell, The Drunken Boat, and Illuminations
By Arthur Rimbaud
Translated by James Sibley Watson, Lionel Abel, and Wallace Fowlie

Print ISBN 13: 978-1-4209-6113-3
eBook ISBN 13: 978-1-4209-6050-1

This edition copyright © 2018. Digireads.com Publishing.

Cover Image: a detail of "A Corner of the Table", c. 1872 (oil on canvas), by Ignace Henri Jean Fantin-Latour (1836-1904) / Musee d'Orsay, Paris, France / Bridgeman Images.

Please visit *www.digireads.com*

# CONTENTS

## Introduction

The whole of Arthur Rimbaud's work, on which poets have "fed", to use the term of Paul Valéry, for some sixty-five years, was completed in four years of adolescence, between the ages of sixteen and twenty.

So Rimbaud was almost magically precocious. However it is not necessary to credit the claim of his brother-in-law and most foolish biographer, Paterne Berrichon, that Rimbaud proceeded to distinguish himself almost immediately after he was born. Such myths should really be discredited; they can only serve to trivialize a life that has become a legend insofar as whatever was extraordinary in it was also meaningful. Precocity was essential to the characteristic genius of Rimbaud; for that very reason it should be taken seriously and not assimilated, as by Berrichon, to nursery lore. Rimbaud, bear in mind, was not simply an exceptional poet considering his youth—like say Chatterton—he was much more remarkable than that. Somehow he was able to utilize his youthfulness and innocence of the world as principles of discovery and origination, as other poets have utilized their experience of life, as Goethe exploited his wisdom, Villon his crimes.

Rimbaud was born in Northern France, in the provinces of the Ardennes. At fifteen, a prize-winning scholar at the Collège de Charleville, with a thorough training in Latin and French literatures, he began to write verses. At sixteen he was already an original poet with a fully developed attitude of antagonism for the values of his environment. He was for poetry, revolution, Paris, against religion, the bourgeoisie and the provinces. The temper of his mind at that time can be seen from the letter he wrote to his schoolmaster, George Izambard, when news came of the first French reverses of the Franco-Prussian war. Rimbaud had nothing but contempt for the agitation of the good bourgeois of the Ardennes. "The blessed people!" he wrote, "these bravos who go about with pat phrases on their lingues act otherwise than the besieged of Metz and Strassbourg. They are frightful; these retired grocers who don their uniforms again. It is sickening, it simply stinks the way these notaries, glaziers, collectors, carpenters, and all those fat bellies with rifles go playing at super-patriotism around the gates of Mezières. My country rises up! Personally I should prefer to see her sitting down. Don't shift your feet, that's my motto. . . . Paris doesn't care what happens to us—not a single new book! This is deadly. . . . A fine spot to be in! I am an exile in my own country!"

He was also an exile in his home. The father, a retired infantry officer of the French colonial army, had abandoned the family and Rimbaud could have seen little of him. The mother, Vitalie Rimbaud, who took charge of the household, was a descendant of great landed proprietors of the provinces, a woman intensely proud and masterful, bigoted, avaricious, and with a horror of bohemianism which was doubtless augmented by her husband's desertion. She had no use for daydreaming, idleness or poetry, and naturally was continually at odds with her son. She even kicked up a row because Izambard lent Rimbaud a copy of Les Misérables, a book on the Index. She was a "strong-willed countrywoman", but in will at least her son resembled her. Rimbaud sold his armful of academic prizes for twenty francs and went off to Paris.

He was arrested on his arrival at the Gare de l'Est and sent back. But he did not stay for long. He was off again shortly, first to Brussels and then twice to Paris. All of these trips ended ignominiously in repentant returns to Charleville.

On the last of these journeys, which Rimbaud undertook on foot and without a penny in his pocket, it may have been his intention to enroll in the Commune. A few days before his departure he wrote to Izambard: "I am going to become a worker. This perspective comforts me when rage and fury urge me towards the battle in Paris where so many workers are dying even while I write to you. But to work now? Never, never! Now I am on strike." Rimbaud had not read Marx but he was familiar with the writings of Rousseau, Helvetius, Mably, Morelly and Babeuf, and according to Delahaye he was engaged at that time in drawing up a constitution for the future communist state. It is not known whether he got to Paris on this trip, and Jean-Marie Carré argues convincingly against the tale that he actually joined the troops of the Revolution. But his sympathy with the rebellion is beyond question, passionately chanted in three marvellous poems, Les Mains de Jeanne-Marie, Chant du Guerre Parisien, and Paris Se Repeuple, that furious diatribe against the Versaillese, which rivals the very best imprecations of Timon and Lear in its ecstasy of hatred. Whether he joined the workers' troops or no Rimbaud was certainly heart and soul with the Commune.

Who in fact could have been a more appropriate celebrator of that adolescent revolution, so naively in advance of historic possibility, than the schoolboy whose literary slogan was: "Poetry must no longer rhythm action—it must go ahead of it"? Then too, Rimbaud and the Revolution were equally victims of the middle-class smugness of the provinces. And as the Commune is the most innocent of all revolutions, going down into history defeated but without crimes, so Rimbaud is the most innocent of poets, if only because his work was completed in adolescence, before he was "mature" enough for adaptation, compromise, the lure of the academy.

The Commune was crushed but poetry was still a value and Paris still attractive even if "repopulated" by the bourgeoisie. Rimbaud wrote to Paul Démeny: "Forever locked up in this indescribable Ardennes country, seeing no one, absorbed as I am in my unsuitable, stupefying, obstinate and mysterious work, answering all questions, all vulgar and wicked reproaches with complete silence, bearing myself as befits my extra-legal position, I have finally brought down on myself the most horrible condemnations of a mother as inflexible as sixty-three helmeted administrations. She wants to condemn me to perpetual hard work in Charleville. Get yourself a job by such and such a date or get out, she said. . . . She has gotten to the point where she wants me to run away. . . . I am willing to work hard, but in Paris, which I love."

The "unsuitable, stupefying, obstinate and mysterious work" referred to here was the rigorous practice of self-hallucination, a technique for inspiring himself which Rimbaud had adopted. In another letter, which has become famous as the Letter of the Seer, Rimbaud explained his method:

"I say that it is necessary to be a *seer,* to make one-self a SEER.

"The poet makes himself a *seer* by means of a long, immense and methodological *derangement* of *all* his *senses.* All forms of love, suffering, madness; he searches himself, he absorbs all poisons in order to retain only their quintessences. Ineffable torment, for which he has need of all faith, all superhuman force, whereby he becomes the great sick man, the great criminal, the greatly cursed,—and the supreme Savant!—For he arrives at the *unknown!*—Since he has cultivated his soul, already richer than anyone's! He arrives at the unknown; and if, maddened, he should lose all intelligence of his visions, at least he has seen them! Let him explode in his plunge among unheard-of, unnameable things: other horrible workers shall come; they shall commence at the very horizons where their predecessor sank!

"Hence the poet is truly a Thief of Fire.

"He is charged with humanity, even with the *animals;* he must make his inventions felt, handled, heard. If what he brings up from *below* has form, he expresses its form; what is without form he exhibits without form. To find a language:

"This language shall be of the soul for the soul, resuming all perfumes, sounds and colors, thought bearing up thought and leading it forwards. The poet should define the quantity of the unknown awaking in his time in the universal soul: he should give more than the formula of his thought, than the notation of his *march to Progress!* Enormity becoming the norm absorbed by all he would be a veritable *multiplicator of progress!*

"The future shall be materialist, you shall see.—Always full of *Number* and *Harmony,* poems shall be made to endure.—Greek Poetry shall have some part in this.

"These poets shall come to be! And when the infinite servitude of woman is liquidated, when she shall live by her own resources and for her own goals—man's until now abominable mastery broken—she also shall become a poet! Women, too, shall discover the unknown! Will their worlds of ideas differ from ours? They shall find strange, unbelievable, reposeful and delicious things which we shall take and understand."

It has been generally assumed that Rimbaud continued to hold to the poetical doctrine elaborated in this letter and that it provided the method for what poetry he wrote afterwards. In a certain sense this is quite true, for Rimbaud continued the practice of self-hallucination and the pursuit of the "unknown" as the special object of imagination. Hut certain nice distinctions must be made. At different stages of his practice the "unknown" has a different content for Rimbaud. The "Letter of the Seer" was written prior to the repression of the Commune and despite its romantic rhetoric of horror contains much that is socially affirmative. Notice that the poet is regarded as a unit in a collectivity of poets and as having a responsible relation to humanity; that his "horrible" work is performed not for his own advantage but for others; that the future is envisaged optimistically, in terms of some kind of progress; that the social liberation of woman is related to progress in the "unknown".

When one compares the poetry Rimbaud wrote prior to or contemporary with the Commune, and Bateau Ivre, written some months after the massacres in Paris, two radically different conceptions of the "unknown" emerge.

The early poems of Rimbaud, those in which he directly celebrated the Commune, and also such poems as Les Premieres Communions, L'Homme Juste, Le Mal, Les Pauvres A L'Eglise, bold demanding chants against all forms of submissiveness and illusion, are not lacking in that *visionary* quality which characterizes Bateau Ivre and the works that followed it. In his early poems Rimbaud's tactic is to astonish and scandalize, or perhaps I should say to astonish *in order* to scandalize. The "unknown" in these poems is not that which is inaccessible by ordinary modes of study, but that which a good bourgeois could not have the moral courage to admit; the "unknown" is the socially monstrous and Rimbaud's method is to bring the reader into intimate relation with this monstrousness and in a state too weakened by marvels of music and imagery for escape. Instances of this type of *seeing* are the image of Christ, yellowed by the stained glass windows, yielding to aesthetic disdain for his miserable worshippers in Les Pauvres A L'Eglise, and God accepting the pennies of weeping mothers in Le Mal.

With Bateau Ivre the entire feeling has changed; the shock of the scandalous disappears, or reappears as a minor scandal of nature in such an image as "snot-blue of the blue"; the scandalous is now an added attraction of the astonishing. Instead of illusion it is now consciousness which is the enemy; the "unknown" is now an attractive natural object in which the poet longs to be anaesthetized.

If one could generalize the content of Bateau Ivre one might describe it as an imaginative experiment in contacting nature without the interference of society. A scenario of the poem would indicate a journey into the universe in the course of which tools and companions are discarded. In the very first stanza the traveller says that his guides have been scalped by Indians and in the second stanza he expresses unconcern for their fate and delight at being alone on the rivers. He goes on into the ocean in a tiny pine shell, devours the waters where drowned men have floated, sees the marvels of immense distances, Leviathan, the colors of the universe, what men believe they see. He becomes so drunk with water that neither Hansa schooners nor the Monitor, symbols of commerce and civil war, can fish him up. Finally he speaks with bitterness of the dawn, of moon and sun. This might appear to contradict the interpretation of the poem I am offering. For dawn, moon and sun are characters of nature, not of society. But the very next verse explains away the contradiction. The traveller complains that harsh love has bloated him with drunken torpors. He wants to drown; but he is kept afloat, he can look up overhead, that is why sun, moon and dawn are odious, and it is harsh love (a marvellous idea!) that buoys him to the surface of the waters. Then comes the cry "May my keel splinter! May I take the sea!" Even the frail pine shell is now felt as an impediment, after all, it too is a product of society. The traveller then declares that he will accept of Europe's waters only some cold black puddle where at twilight a child might sail a tiny boat. (Some delicate perfume of European life as a sort of last whisper to be retained on this journey into the world.) In the last verse he says he can no longer swim in the proximity of ships, flags, or barges with horrible eyes. Some commentator has suggested that by "barges with horrible eyes" Rimbaud may have meant to designate the prison convoys, perhaps those carrying off the revolutionaries arrested by Thiers.

Taking a friend's advice Rimbaud sent off a copy of Bateau Ivre to Paul Verlaine, one of the few contemporary poets he admired. Two weeks later he received an enthusiastic letter from Verlaine inviting him to Paris.

But Rimbaud soon found the literary circles in Paris as insufferable as the bourgeois life of the Ardennes. He must himself have been insufferable with his provincial awkwardness, systematic rudeness and terrible pride. He still maintained a severe conception of the poet's role and neither Verlaine nor Verlaine's friends could measure up to it. They certainly were not "thieves of fire". Rimbaud felt an immense superiority to everyone he met, but nobody acknowledged this superiority, nobody, that is, except Verlaine. Finally Rimbaud persuaded Verlaine to leave his wife, who was expecting a child, and go wandering with him through Belgium and England, promising ironically, to restore Verlaine "to his original condition as a child of the sun".

For more than two years they adventured together in bohemian vagabondage, "dining on wine of the dens and biscuit of the roads". There was, of course, an essential misunderstanding in their relationship. To Verlaine's accommodating, feminine nature, bewitched by Rimbaud's "mysterious delicacies", their bohemian life meant self-indulgence, moral softness, relaxation; while for Rimbaud it was the necessary condition for ignoring the bourgeois world he despised and for the rigorous practice of self-hallucination, the poetical hygiene which he had substituted for conventional morality.

It was during his wanderings with Verlaine that Rimbaud composed most of Les Illuminations. Still another variant of the "unknown" is pursued in these strange, solitary, uncommunicating poems. Critics have been struck by their "objectivity". For Jacques Rivière they are notations of some "immense body", descriptions of a metaphysical object, shorthand quotations of the absolute; for Etiemble and Gauclère they are objective in a Bergsonian sense, being descriptions of things-in-themselves undistorted by spacializing and variable human perspectives.

I do not see how any critic could better the qualitative analysis of Les Illuminations made by Jacques Rivière in his brilliant if theologically mystified study of Rimbaud. Rivière points out the "unsociable" character of Les Illuminations; rhyme is omitted in most of them not because rhyme is an old-fashioned technical device to be substituted for by some other mode of resonance, but because rhyme has a conversational significance and organizes the *reply* of one section of a poem to another, facilitates the friendliness of distant elements; while in Les Illuminations "everything is parallel; or rather everything is successive". "The style of Rimbaud is the style of someone who seeks to attain something no matter how."

What is it that Rimbaud was seeking to attain no matter how in Les Illuminations? Like the other French symbolist poets of the late nineteenth century, Rimbaud was concerned, in the absence of a transformation of society, to transform his own ego, to empty it of those desires which it could not satisfy in bourgeois life, to throw out of it; psychic sphere citizenship, morality, sentiment, and limit it as a specialized aesthetic field for the hallucinatory exchanges of words, symbols, sensations, ideas. But what differentiated Rimbaud from such a symbolist as Mallarmé was that for Rimbaud the end term of this typical psychic transformation was not literature but life; "changing life" was the slogan, as Rimbaud indicated in Une Saison En Enfer, of

Les Illuminations. These poems were not intended as artistic commodities to be enjoyed by others, they were not ends but procedures, exercises in a hygiene of sensibility; they have the "objectivity" and "unsociability" of personal exercises. They are sighs, organic whispers, adorable goodbyes, improvised lusts, ritual refinements and scandals of sensation, sheer verbal abracadabra: the "unknown" solicited in the orders of sensation and of language. "I tried to invent," Rimbaud wrote of these poems, "new stars, new flowers, new flesh, new tongues." All delicately calculated towards the achievement of a magical immunity to the demands of bourgeois life: work, boredom, unscrupulousness. Prideful efforts to act like an angel, say the Catholic critics.

Rimbaud expected something of poetry; a better life, and this of course it was unable to provide him with. Hunger and humiliation together with dreams were insufficient to his pride. Even a *verbal* immunity to the pressures of bourgeois life, he came to realize, was impossible of attainment: "The old poetic rubbish played an important role in my alchemy of the word." And his poverty made it necessary for him to confront reality with an unhallucinated consciousness. If Rimbaud had had independent means the limitations of imagining might not have appeared so absolute. But fate had chosen by rendering him helpless, with a mother who had a horror of his talents, to utilize him as an extreme instance of the incompatibility in a capitalist civilization of the practical and the poetic. After two years of wandering with Verlaine, Rimbaud was a "tired" poet, a phenomenon less familiar than the "tired" radical only because poets so seldom make radical demands on their art. His dissatisfaction with poetry must have made him hate Verlaine, who was incapable of anything but poetry, and Rimbaud finally parted company with him in Brussels; but only after Verlaine had shot him in the wrist for threatening to leave, been arrested, and sentenced to eighteen months imprisonment.

Rimbaud returned to his mother's home in the Ardennes. Physically sick, spiritually exhausted, he nevertheless locked himself at once in his room and working sometimes twenty-four hours at a stretch composed his "nigger" book of "innocence", Une Saison En Enter. In this work, a spiritual autobiography written in that "diamond-like" prose which Verlaine said was his exclusive gift, Rimbaud mercilessly analyzed the poetry he had written and the kind of life it had involved: "I believed in all the spells of magic." "I accustomed myself to simple hallucinations." Poetry had led him to base a whole existence on methodological superstitiousness with regard to the power of words; "then I explained my magical sophistries with the hallucination of words! I ended by consecrating the disorder of my brain." The weakened egotism of a hallucinated life was contemptible: "Let us make believe, let us be idle, O Pity! And we shall live for our own amusement, dreaming monstrous loves and fantastic universes, continually whining and carping at the actual face of the world, acrobat, beggar, artist, bandit—priest!" Hut if poetry was to be rejected, was there any superior form of consciousness to be had in Europe? "Science does not move fast enough." Religion? "I shall not embark on a honeymoon with Jesus Christ for a father-in-law." The whole superstructure of European civilization was hellish, stimulating the ego and leaving it dissatisfied. And here Rimbaud returned to that desirable "unknown" of nature, conceived with so much ecstasy in Bateau Ivre. Hut this time Rimbaud was more realistic, the flight into nature would only be a second best. It was now "the march, the burden, the desert, ennui and anger." It would involve silencing the spirit, consciousness, sensibility: "Finding that I have two pennies left of common sense— which is quickly spent!—I see that my unhappiness comes from having ignored too long that we are in the Occident. The Occidental swamps! . . . My two poor pennies of common sense are spent. The spirit is authority. It asks me to remain in the Occident. I must silence the spirit to conclude as I have proposed."

Having published Une Saison En Enfer in Brussels and then burned every copy of it he could lay hands on, together with the rest of his writings, Rimbaud set about preparing himself to abandon Europe. He devoted himself to a systematic study of all languages useful for trade or travel, English, German, Spanish, Italian, Russian, Greek, Arabic. Then came five long, miserable years of invariably frustrated attempts to reach the East. Once Rimbaud even enlisted in the Dutch army to get to Java, but deserted at Batavia and came back home again. On different occasions he got to Stockholm, Hamburg, Vienna, and Cyprus, where he contracted typhoid fever, only to have to return each time to Charleville. But he was now as obstinate about quitting Europe as he had formerly been to reach the center of its aesthetic consciousness, Paris. Finally he got to Aden where he landed a job with a French firm of coffee importers. Then he went into business for himself at Harrar, trading in sugar, rice, silk and guns. He had dealings with Menelik, the King of Abyssinia, who is said to have been too shrewd for him and to have swindled him outrageously. At last, after twelve years of hardship and commercial intrigues, as a result of which he had little to show in the way of profit, and which had so depreciated his pride that now his one ambition was to make enough money to return to Europe and marry a French girl, (she would bear him a son, he said, whom he would educate so that the boy might grow great and powerful through *science)* Rimbaud found himself physically disabled. He was afflicted with a swelling in the leg and had to be carried on a litter to Aden. Then he was shipped to Marseille where his leg was amputated. But the infection, whatever it was, had already affected his whole system. So he went back to Charleville, a "terrible invalid" returned from "the hot lands", a "great sick man" indeed, but stricken not with the deliberately cultivated disorders he had planned for himself long years before, but with an accidentally contracted ailment of the body; a kind of ironical retaliation of nature for his having attempted to escape from the disasters of the mind. Rimbaud spent an agonized summer at Charleville, and then, hoping desperately to return to the East, went back, attended by his sister to Marseille. He died there in the Hospital of the Immaculate Conception, ending his life, says his sister, "in a sort of continual dream . . . mixing up all sorts of things with art".

Very much in the style of his early poetry directed against capitalist society, this unhappy life of Arthur Rimbaud astonishes and scandalizes. That he was great before he was grown up is a miracle of nature, that he calculated his adult existence on a deliberate refusal to be great is a perfect scandal to society. Thus Rimbaud's life violently disrupts our categories of admiration. We are accustomed to thinking of a significant life as one that evolves from a lower to a higher order, instancing some definite acquisition for the human spirit. And Rimbaud compels us to admire against this bias, to marvel at a falling off, a backsliding and depletion, a regression from the civilized to the primitive, from poetry to prose, from prose to silence; he compels us to acclaim a rejection and disparagement of culture. Is it not a scandal for a poet to have exposed the radical insufficiency of the most perfect type of speech, chief pride and glory of the human spirit?

It is very difficult, in view of our inveterate pragmatism, to admit that someone has been great to nobody's advantage. But if bourgeois culture has not been aggrandized by the genius and misfortunes of Rimbaud, yet cannot God find profit in them? Yes, indeed, says Jacques Rivière, who holds that Rimbaud was a sort of eccentric agent of the supernatural, "almost without metaphor", an angel, that his mission was precisely to disorient and indict humanity, to expose its limitedness, to disparage culture and science, and destroy all forms of solidarity. In the interest, be it understood, of the Christian God.

It will not be worth while to argue here against so frankly metaphysical a hypothesis, for proof of which Rivière can adduce nothing but eloquence. Is it not more plausible to observe that the human spirit and life itself are so intimately involved with existing forms of social organization, that to totally indict the society in which one lives, unless some drastic change is imminent or expected, is to indict the human spirit and life as well? Conversely all victorious adjustments of the human spirit, no matter how fortunate, reflect some glory on the society that supported or permitted them. If, then, Arthur Rimbaud appears like an enemy of life and culture, it is only because he was a frustrated enemy of the bourgeoisie. He seems to have tried to disorient all relations because he could not succeed in disorienting bourgeois relations, he seems to discourage all forms of human solidarity because he himself tried to dispense with bourgeois forms of solidarity. He is symbolic of the frustrated spirit in our time as Goethe instanced the spirit's capacity for consummation at the beginning of the bourgeois era. We do not disparage Goethe because his long, tranquil, masterfully equilibrated career does not horrify us with the bourgeois world we live in. With equal justice, all honor, then, to Arthur Rimbaud, whose brief, prodigious, mutilated existence does not make us glad to be alive.

LIONEL ABEL.

## A Season in Hell

### Translated by J. S. Watson, Jr.

Once on a time, if I remember rightly, my life was a feast where all hearts opened and every wine ran.

One evening I set Beauty on my knees.—And I found her sour.—And I cursed her.

I took arms against justice.

I fled. O sorcerers, misery, and hatred, it is to you my treasure has been entrusted!

I was able to obliterate from my mind all human hope. Upon each joy, to strangle it, I made the soundless spring of a wild beast.

I called the executioners that, dying, I might bite the butts of their guns. I called the scourges to choke me with sand, with blood. Misfortune was my god. I stretched myself out in the mud. I dried myself in the air of crime. And I played folly some good tricks.

And Spring brought me the frightful laugh of an idiot.

Now, just lately, finding I was on the edge of giving my last gasp, it occurred to me to look for the key to the ancient feast, where I might perhaps find appetite again.

Charity is that key.—An inspiration which proves that I have been dreaming.

"You shall remain a hyena, etc. . . ." shrieks the fiend who crowned me with such amiable poppies. "Earn death with all your appetites and your egoism and all the capital offenses."

Ah! I have taken too much of it:—But, dear Satan, I beg you a less petulant eye! and while awaiting the several little misdeeds in arrears, you who admire in a writer the absence of all that might be descriptive or edifying, I detach for your benefit these few hideous pages from my damned man's diary.

### BAD BLOOD

From my Gallic ancestors I get my pale blue eyes, narrow skull and awkwardness in fight. I find my costume as barbarous as theirs. Only I do not butter my hair.

The Gauls were the clumsiest beast-flayers and grass-burners of their time.

From them I get: idolatry and love of sacrilege;—Oh! all the vices, rage, sensuality—magnificent sensuality;—above all dying and laziness.

I have a horror of all trades. Masters or workmen, all peasants, low-born. The hand at the pen is no worse than the hand at the plow,—

and no better. What a century for hands! I will never have my hand.
After that, family life leads too far. The propriety of begging wounds
me to death. Criminals are disgusting like geldings; as for me, I am
intact, and don't care.

But! who made my tongue so deceitful that up to now it has guided
and guarded my laziness? Without having earned my bread even with
my body, lazier than a toad, I have lived everywhere. Not a family of
Europe that I do not know.—I mean families like my own which hold
everything from the declaration of the Rights of Man.—I have known
every son of a family!

If I had antecedents at any point whatever in French history!

But no, nothing.

It is perfectly evident to me that I have always belonged to the
under race. I cannot comprehend rebellion. My people never rose
except to pillage: so wolves the animal they have not killed.

I call to mind the history of France, eldest daughter of the Church.
As a *vilain* I must have made the journey to the Holy Land; I have in
my head routes in the Suabian plain, views of Byzantium, of the
ramparts of Solyma; the cult of Mary, the yearning over the Crucified,
awake in me among a thousand profane fairy tales.—I am seated
among broken pots and nettles, leprous, at the bottom of a wall gnawed
by the sun.—Later, to continue, I must have bivouacked under
Germany's nights.

Ah! again: I dance the sabbath in a red clearing with old women
and children.

I do not remember myself farther back than this country and
Christianity. I shall "never finish seeing myself again in this past. But
alone always, with no family: what language did I use to speak, even? I
never see myself at the councils of Christ; nor at the councils of the
Lords,—the representatives of Christ.

What was I in the last century? I do not find myself again till
today. No more migrations, no more vague wars. The under race has
overrun everything—the people, as they say, reason, the nation, and
science.

Oh! science! They have reclaimed it all. For the body and for the
soul—the viaticum—they have medicine and philosophy—old
women's remedies and popular songs rearranged. And the amusements
of the princes and the games they used to forbid. Geography,
cosmography, mechanics, chemistry! . . .

Science, the new nobility! Progress. The world advances! Why
should it not turn?

It is the vision of numbers. We are on our way to the *Spirit*. It is
quite certain, it is oracular, what I say. I understand, and as I do not
know how to explain myself without pagan words, I wish to be silent.

The pagan blood returns! The Spirit is near; why does Christ not help me by giving my soul nobility and freedom? Alas, the Gospel has gone by! the Gospel! the Gospel.

I await God greedily. I belong to the under race for all eternity.

Here I am on the Breton coast. The cities light up at evening. My day's work is done; I am leaving Europe. The sea air shall burn my lungs; lost climates shall tan me. Swim, pound roots, hunt, above all smoke; drink liquor strong as boiling metal,—as those dear ancestors of mine did formerly round their fires!

I will return with limbs of iron, dark-skinned, furious-eyed; from my mask they shall think me of a strong race. I will have money: I will be indolent and brutal. Women tend these terrible invalids back from the hot countries. I will get mixed up in politics. Saved!

Now I am outcast, I have a horror of my country. The best thing would be sleep, quite drunk, on the beach.

You don't go—Reenter the old ways here, loaded down with my vice, the vice which has sent its roots of suffering into my side ever since the age of reason,—which towers to the sky, strikes me, knocks me down, drags me along.

Last innocence and last timidity. It is said. Not bring my disgusts and betrayals to the world.

Come! The march, the burden, the desert, ennui and anger.

To whom am I to hire myself out? What animal must be adored? What holy image assaulted? What hearts shall I break? What lie ought I to hold to?—In what blood walk?

Rather keep myself clear of the law.—A hard life, a plain self-stultification,—lift with withered fist the lid of the coffin, sit down, suffocate. In this way be rid of old age and dangers: fear is not French.

—Ah! I am so weary that I offer my impulses toward perfection to no matter what divine image.

O my self-abnegation, my marvelous charity! down here, however.

*De profundis. Domine,* am I a fool!

While still a child I used to admire the incurable malefactor upon whom the prison hulks shut forever; I visited the inns and lodgings that he might have consecrated by his sojourn; I saw with his *idea* the blue sky and the flowered work of the country; I used to scent his fatality in the cities. He had more strength than a saint, more good sense than a traveller—and he, he alone! as witness of his glory and of his rightness.

On the high-roads, winter nights, shelterless, unclothed, without bread, a voice clenched my frozen heart: "Weakness or strength: you see, it is strength. You know neither where you are going nor why you go; enter everywhere, respond to all. They will not kill you any more than if you were a corpse." In the morning I had so lost a gaze, and a face so dead, that the people whom I met perhaps *did not see me.*

In the cities the mud seemed to me suddenly red and black, like a mirror when the lamp moves in the next room, like a treasure in the forest! "Good luck," I cried, and I saw a sea of flame and smoke up to heaven, and right and left all wealth blazing like a billion thunderstorms.

But debauchery and the companionship of women were forbidden me. Not even a comrade. I used to see myself before the angry crowd, confronting the cordon of executioners, weeping over their inability to understand, and forgiving them!—Like Jeanne d'Arc!—"Priests, professors, school masters, you are wrong to turn me over to justice. I have never belonged to this people; I have never been a Christian; I belong to the race that sang in punishment. I do not under- stand, and forgiving them!—Like Jeanne d'Arc!—beast: you are making a blunder,"

Yes, my eyes are shut to your light. I am a brute, a negro. But I can be saved. You are false negroes, you, maniacs, savages, misers. You, merchant, are a negro; you, magistrate, a negro; you, general, a negro; emperor, old itch, you are a negro: you have drunk untaxed liquor of Satan's manufacture.—This people is inspired by fever and cancer. Invalids and old men are so respectable that they demand boiling. The spite-fullest thing would be to quit this continent where madness prowls in search of hostages for these wretches. I am going to the true kingdom of the children of Ham.

Did I still know nature? Did I know myself?—*No more words.* I bury the dead in my belly. Shouts, drum, dance, dance, dance, dance! I do not even see the hour when the whites will disembark and I shall fall into nothingness.

Hunger, thirst, shouts, dance, dance, dance, dance!

The whites are landing. The cannon! You must submit to baptism, put on clothes, work.

I have felt the finishing stroke at my heart. Ah! I had not expected it!

I have never done evil. My days are going to be easy, I shall be spared repentance. I shall not have endured the tortures of the soul almost dead to virtue, in whom the severe light comes back to life like funeral candles. The lot of the son of the house, premature coffin covered with limpid tears. Without doubt debauchery is stupid, vice is stupid; filth must be thrown away. But the clock will not have arrived at the point of striking no hour but that of pure woe. Am I going to be carried off like a child to play in paradise, forgetful of all unhappiness?

Quick! are there other lives? Sleep in wealth is impossible. Wealth has always been very public. Divine love alone can provide the keys of knowledge. I see that nature is nothing but a display of goodness. Farewell, chimeras, ideals, errors!

The reasonable hymn of the angels rises from the ship of salvation: it is divine love.—Two loves! I can die of earthly love, die of devoutness. I have left souls behind whose grief will grow at my departure. You choose me from among the shipwrecked; those who remain, are they not my friends?

Save them!

Reason is born in me. The world is good. I will bless life. I will love my brothers. These are no longer childish promises. Nor the hope of escaping old age and death. God is my strength, and I praise God.

I am no longer in love with disgust. Rage, debauchery, folly— whose every impulse and disaster I know-all my burden is laid aside. Consider without reeling the extent of my innocence.

I should no longer be able to ask for the solace of a bastinado. I do not fancy myself embarked on a wedding with Jesus Christ for father-in-law.

I am not the prisoner of my reason. I have said: God. I want freedom in salvation: how am I to seek it? Frivolous inclinations have left me. No more need of devotions or of God's love. I do not regret the century of impressionable hearts. Every one to his own reason, contempt, and charity. I retain my place at the top of this angelic ladder of good sense.

As for settled happiness, domestic or not . . . no, I am incapable of it. I am too dissipated, too weak. Life blooms through work, old truism; my life is not heavy enough, it soars and floats high above action, that dear pivot of the world.

What an old maid I am becoming, to lack the courage to be in love with death!

If God granted me the heavenly, aerial quietude of prayer,—like that of the ancient saints.—The saints, strong men! The hermits, artists such as we have need of no longer!

Continual farce? My innocence would make me weep. Life is the farce to lead everywhere.

Enough! here is chastisement.—*March!*

Ah! my lungs burn, my temples roar! Night rolls through my eyes in this sunlight! Heart . . . limbs

Where are we going to bathe? I am weak! the others advance. Tools, weapons . . . time . . .

Fire, fire on me! There! or I surrender.—Cowards!—I kill myself! I throw myself under the horses' hoofs!

Ah!. . .

—I shall get used to it.

This would be the French life, the path of honour!

## NIGHT IN HELL

I have swallowed a famous throatful of poison.—Thrice blest be the counsel that came to me.—My bowels broil. The shock of the poison twists my limbs, distorts me, throws me to earth. I am dying of thirst, suffocating, I cannot cry out. It is hell, it is the everlasting torment. See how the fire blazes up! I am burning properly. Away, demon!

I had caught a glimpse of my conversion to virtue and happiness, my salvation. Can I describe the vision? The atmosphere of hell is not congenial to hymns. There were millions of charming creatures, a bland concert of spirits, strength and peace, noble ambitions, I know not what else.

Noble ambitions!

And this is life still!—Suppose damnation were eternal! A man who wants to mutilate himself is quite damned, is he not? I believe that I am in hell, therefore I am. It is the catechism at work. I am the slave of my baptism. Parents, you contrived my misfortune and your own. Poor innocent!—Hell cannot touch the heathen.—This is life still. Later the delights of damnation will be more profound. A crime, quick, and I fall into nothingness beyond the laws of men.

Silence, there, silence! Shame, reproach here: Satan who says the fire is mean, my rage appallingly out of place.—Enough! . . . Of the errors they deplore in me, magic, false perfumes, childish tunes.—And they tell me that I hold the truth, that I perceive justice: I have a sane, well-bridled judgment, I am ready for perfection. . . . Pride.—My scalp is parched. Pity! Lord, I am afraid. I am thirsty, so thirsty. Ah! childhood, the grass, the rain, the lake on the pebbles, *the full moon when the clock was striking twelve.* . The devil is in the belfry at this hour. Mary! Holy Virgin! . . .—Horror at my inanity.

Out there, are those not honest souls who wish me well? . . . Help . . . I have a pillow on my mouth, they do not hear me, they are phantoms. Besides, no one ever thinks of others. Let them keep off. I smell of seared flesh, like a heretic; there is no doubt about it.

The hallucinations are innumerable. Just what I have always had; no more faith in history, forgetfulness of principles. I will keep them to myself; poets and visionaries might be jealous. We are a thousand times the richest; let us be close-fisted like the sea.

There! a moment ago the clock of life stopped. I am no longer in the world. Theology is serious, hell is certainly *down below,*—and heaven above.—Ecstasy, nightmare, sleep in a nest of flames.

What tricks of attention in the country . . . Satan, Ferdinand, runs with the wild grain . . . Jesus walks on the purple briers, without their bending. Jesus was walking on the angry waters. The lantern showed him to us standing, white with brown locks, on the flank of an emerald wave. . . .

I am going to unveil all the mysteries: mysteries of religion or of nature, death, birth, future, past, cosmogony, nonexistence. I am master of phantasmagoria.

Listen! . .

I have all the talents!—There is nobody here, and there is somebody. I should not care to squander my treasure.—Do you want negro songs, houri dances? Do you want me to vanish, to plunge after the *ring?* Do you? I will make gold, remedies.

Trust in me, then; faith assuages, guides, cures. All, come,—even little children, that I may console you, that his heart may be poured out for you like water,—the marvellous heart!—Poor human beings, toilers! I do not ask you for prayers; with your faith alone I shall be happy.

And think of me. This makes me barely regret the world. I have a chance of not suffering any more. My life consisted of mild follies only, it is to be regretted.

Bah! make all the grimaces imaginable!

Decidedly we are out of the world. No longer any sound. The sense of touch has left me. Ah! my castle, my Saxony, my wood of willow trees. Evenings, mornings, nights, days. . . . Am I tired!

I ought to have my hell for anger, my hell for pride,—and the hell of laziness; a concert of hells.

I am dying of lassitude. It is the grave. I am going to the worms, horror of horrors! Satan, you clown, you want to dissolve me with your charms. I demand. I demand! a fork-thrust, a drop of fire.

Ah! climb back to life! Gaze at our deformities. And this poison, this kiss a thousand times accursed! My weakness, the cruelty of the world! My God, pity, hide me, I am too ill!—I am hidden and I am not.

It is the fire waking again with its damned.

DELIRES I. FOOLISH VIRGIN—THE INFERNAL BRIDEGROOM

Hear the confession of a companion in Hell: "O heavenly Bridegroom, my Lord, do not deny the confession of the most unhappy of thy servants. I am lost. I am drunken. I am unclean. What a life!

"Forgive me, heavenly Lord, forgive me! Ah! forgive me! what tears! And what tears again, later on, I trust!

"Later on I shall know the heavenly Bridegroom! I was born subject to Him.—The other can beat me now!

"At present, I am at the bottom of the world, O my friends! . . . no, not my friends. . . . Never delirium nor torture to equal these. . . . Is it ridiculous!

"Ah! I suffer, I cry out. I suffer truly. Nevertheless all is allowed me, loaded with the contempt of the most contemptible hearts.

"At any rate let me make this avowal, free to repeat it twenty other times,—as depressing, as insignificant!

"I am the slave of the infernal Bridegroom, the one who ruined the foolish virgins. It is surely that same demon. It is not a ghost, not a phantom. But I, who have lost my wisdom, who am damned and dead to the world—they will not kill me! How describe him to you! I no longer know how to talk even. I am in black, I weep, I am afraid. A little freshness, Lord, if you will, if you will well.

"I am a widow . . .—I used to be a widow . . .—why yes, I was perfectly respectable at one time, and I was not born to become a skeleton! . . . He was almost a child. . . . His mysterious delicacies had led me astray. I forgot my every human duty to follow him. What a life! Real life is absent. We are no longer in the world. I go where he goes, it is necessary. And often he grows furious at me, *me, poor soul.* The Demon!—He is a demon, you know, *he is not a man.*

"He says: 'I do not care for women: love must be reinvented, that's understood. They can do no more than desire a snug situation. When they have it, heart and beauty are discarded; the only thing that is left is cold contempt, the rations of marriage, nowadays. Or else I see women, clearly marked for happiness, whom I might have made into good comrades, devoured first by brutes as tender-hearted as a pile of faggots. . . .!'

"I listen to him making shame a glory, cruelty a charm, 'I belong to a far-off race: my ancestors were Norsemen: they used to pierce their sides, drink their blood. I will make gashes all over my body, I will tattoo myself; I want to grow hideous like a Mongol: you shall see, I will bellow through the streets. I want to grow quite mad with rage. Never show me any jewels, I should grovel and go into contortions on the carpet. My wealth, I want it stained with blood all over. Never will I work. . . .' On several nights, becoming possessed of his demon, we rolled one another about, I fought with him!—Often at night, when he is drunk, he lies in wait for me in the streets or in the house to frighten me to death.—'They will actually cut off my neck; it will be disgusting.' Oh! those days when he wants to walk with an air of crime!

"Sometimes he speaks in a sort of tender child's talk, of death that brings repentance, of the miserable wretches there must be, of grievous toil, of farewells that rend the heart. In the stews where we used to get drunk, he would weep as he watched the people round us, the live stock of squalor. He picked up drunkards out of the black streets. He had a bad mother's pity for little children.—He would move winsomely like a little girl at the catechism.—He would pretend to be informed about everything, business, art, medicine. I followed him, it was necessary.

"I was witness to all the adornment with which he surrounded himself in spirit; garments, cloths, furniture; I lent him weapons, a different face. I saw all that touched him, just as he would have liked to create it for himself. When his spirit seemed to me apathetic, I followed him far in strange and complicated actions, good or bad; I was certain never to enter his world. Beside his dear, sleeping body, what hours I have watched at night, seeking to learn why he was so anxious to escape from reality. Never was there a man with such a vow as that. I recognized,—without being afraid for him,—that he might be a serious danger to society.—Perhaps he possesses secrets that *will change life.* No, I replied to myself, he is only looking for them. Finally his kindness is enchanted, and I am its prisoner. No other soul would have the strength,—the strength of despair!—to endure it, to be loved and protected by him. Besides, I would not picture him to myself with another soul: one sees his Angel, never another's Angel,—I believe. I used to exist in his soul as in a palace which they have made empty in order not to see so mean a person as yourself: that was all. Alas! I was very dependent on him. But what did he want of my colourless and facile being? He would not improve me, unless he were to make me die. Sadly mortified, I sometimes would say to him:

"'I understand you.' He would shrug his shoulders.

"Thus, with my vexation renewing itself daily, finding myself more and more altered in my own eyes—as in all eyes which might have cared to look at me, had I not been condemned everlastingly to the oblivion of all men!—I grew hungrier and hungrier for Ills kindness. With his kisses and friendly embraces, it was indeed a heaven, a gloomy heaven, which I entered, and where I should have wished to be left, poor, deaf, dumb, blind. Already I had the habit of it. I used to see us as good children, free to walk in the Paradise of sadness. We were in harmony with one another. Much affected, we would work together. But after a poignant caress, he would say: 'How funny it will seem to you when I am no longer here, through whom you have passed. When you no longer have my arms under your neck, nor my heart to fall asleep on, nor this mouth upon your eyes. For I shall have to go away, very far, some day. Besides, I must help others; it is my duty. Although this may not be at all appetizing to you . . . dear soul.' All at once I foresaw myself, with him gone, the prey of dizziness, plunged into the most frightful shadow: death. I used to make him promise that he would not abandon me. He gave it twenty times, that lover's promise. It was as frivolous as my saying to him:

"'I understand you.'

"Ah! I have never been jealous of him. He will not leave me, I think. What will happen? He has no connections; he will never do any work. He wants to live like a somnambulist. Will his kindness and charity alone give him rights in the world of the real? At times I forget the trouble into which I have fallen: he shall make me strong, we will travel, we will hunt in the deserts, we will sleep on the pavement of unknown cities, care-free, exempt from pain. Or I will wake up, and the laws and customs shall have changed,—thanks to his magic power; or the world, while remaining the same, shall leave me to my desires, pleasures, unconcerns. Oh! the life of adventure which exists in children's books, to comfort me for all I have suffered, will you give it me? He cannot. I am in the dark as to his ideal. He has told me that he has regrets, aspirations: that should not concern me. Does he talk to God? Perhaps I ought to appeal to God. I am at the very bottom of the abyss, and no longer know how to pray.

"If he were to explain his sorrows to me, should I understand them more than his mockeries? He attacks me, spends hours in making me ashamed of everything in the world which could have touched me, and becomes indignant if I weep.

"'You see that polished young man, stepping into the beautiful calm house yonder: his name is Duval, Dufour, Armand, Maurice, I know not what? A woman has given her life up to loving the wicked idiot: she is dead, a saint in heaven certainly, at present. You would be the death of me, just as he was the death of that woman. It is our fate, we charitable hearts. . .' Alas! there were days when the actions of all men made them seem to him the playthings of a grotesque delirium; he would laugh frightfully, for a long time.—Then, he would resume his ways of a young mother, of an elder sister. If he were less wild, we should be saved. But his tenderness also is deadly. I am subject to him.—Ah! I am foolish!

"One day, perhaps, he will vanish miraculously; but if he is to be taken up again into a heaven, I cannot fail to know, to look on in some measure at the assumption of my little friend!"

Peculiar household!

## DELIRES II. ALCHEMY OF THE WORD

About me. Story of one of my follies.

For a long time I had boasted that I possessed all possible landscapes, and had laughed at the reputations of modern painting and poetry.

I was in love with crazy paintings, over-doors, decorations, tumbler's back-drops, signs, coloured prints; out of date literature, church Latin, lewd books without spelling, the novels of our ancestors, fairytales, little books for children, old librettos, silly refrains, naive rhythms.

I used to dream crusades, voyages of discovery of which we have no account, republics without a history, religious wars nipped in the bud, revolutions in custom, dislodgment of races and of continents: I believed in all the spells of magic.

I invented the colours of the vowels! . . . A black, E white, I red, O blue, U green.—I determined the form and movement of every consonant, and with the aid of instinctive rhythms, I flattered myself that I had invented a poetic language, which would one day or another be accessible to all the senses. I reserved the right of translation.

At first it was a sort of research. I would write silences, nights; I noted the inexpressible. I used to fixate vertigoes.

> Loin des oiseaux, des troupeaux, des villageoises,
> Que buvais-je, à genoux dans cette bruyère
> Entourée de tendres bois de noisetiers,
> Dans un brouillard d'après-midi tiède et vert?
> Que pouvais-je boire dans cette jeune Oise,
> —Ormeaux sans voix, gazon sans fleurs, ciel couvert!—
> Boire à ces gourdes jaunes, loin de ma case
> Chérie? Quelque liqueur d'or qui fait suer.
>
> Je faisais une louche enseigne d'auberge.
> —Un orage vint chasser le ciel. Au soir
> L'eau des bois se perdait sur les sables vierges,
> Le vent de Dieu jetait des glaçons aux mares;
> Pleurant, je voyais de l'or,—et ne pus boire.—
>
> À quatre heures du matin, l'été,
> Le sommeil d'amour dure encore.
> Sous les bocages s'évapore
>     L'odeur de soir fêté.
> Là-bas, dans leur vaste chantier,
> Au soleil des Hespérides,
> Déjà s'agitent—en bras de chemise—
>     Les Charpentiers.
>
> Dans leurs Déserts de mousse, tranquilles,
> Ils préparent les lambris précieux
>     Où la ville
> Peindra de faux cieux.
>
> O, pour ces Ouvriers, charmants
> Sujets d'un roi de Babylone,
> Vénus! quitte un instant les Amants
>     Dont l'âme est en couronne!

      O Reine des Bergers,
      Porte aux travailleurs l'eau-de-vie
      Que leurs forces soient en paix
        En attendant le bain dans la mer à midi.

The old tricks of poetry played an important part in my alchemy of the Word.

I accustomed myself to plain hallucination: quite frankly I used to see a mosque in place of a factory, a school of drums made by angels, carriages on the roads of heaven, a parlour at the bottom of a lake, monsters, mysteries; a ballad title raised up terrors before me.

Then I explained my magical sophistries with the hallucination of words!

I ended by deeming holy the confusion of my mind. I was lazy, prey to a sluggish fever: I envied animals their contentment,— caterpillars which symbolize the innocence of limbo, moles, the sleep of virginity.

My nature became embittered. I said good-bye to the world in kinds of romances:

### CHANSON DE LA PLUS HAUTE TOUR

      Qu'il vienne, qu'il vienne,
      Le temps dont on s'éprenne.

      J'ai tant fait patience
      Qu'à jamais j'oublie.
      Craintes et souffrances
      Aux cieux sont parties.
      Et la soif malsaine
      Obscurcit mes veines.

      Qu'il vienne, qu'il vienne,
      Le temps dont on s'éprenne.

      Telle la prairie
      A l'oubli livrée
      Grandie, et fleurie
      D'encens et d'ivraies,
      Au bourdon farouche
      De très sales mouches

      Qu'il vienne, qu'il vienne,
      Le temps dont on s'éprenne.

I was fond of desert land, burnt orchards, shopworn merchandise, tepid drinks. I dragged myself through stinking alleys, and with eyes shut, offered myself to the sun, the fire god.

"General, if there is still an old cannon left on your ramparts in ruins, bombard us with dried blocks of earth. Before the mirrors of the splendid shops! In the salons! Make the town eat its dust. Oxidize the gargoyles. Fill the boudoirs with the burning powder of rubies. . . ."

Oh! the little fly drunk at the tavern urinal, amorous of borage, and which a ray of light dissolves!

### FAIM

Si j'ai du goût, ce n'est guère
Que pour la terre et les pierres.
Je déjeune toujours d'air,
De roc, de charbons, de fer.

Mes faims, tournez. Paissez, faims,
  Le pré des sons.
Attirez le gai venin
  Des liserons.

Mangez les cailloux qu'on brise,
Les vieilles pierres d'églises;
Les galets des vieux déluges,
Pains semés dans les vallées grises.

Le loup criait sous les feuilles
En crachant les belles plumes
De son repas de volailles:
Comme lui je me consume.

  Les salades, les fruits
N'attendent que la cueillette;
Mais l'araignée de la haie
Ne mange que des violettes.

Que je dorme! que je bouille
  Aux autels de Salomon.
Le bouillon court sur la rouille,
  Et se mêle au Cédron.

At length, O happiness, O reason, I stripped away the sky's azure, which is blackness, and lived, gold spark of the radiance *nature*. From joy I began to wear an expression of comic and complete derangement.

> Elle est retrouvée!
> Quoi? l'Éternité.
> C'est la mer mêlée
>     Au soleil.

> Mon âme éternelle,
> Observe ton voeu
> Malgré la nuit seule
> Et le jour en feu.

> Donc tu te dégages
> Des humains suffrages,
> Des communs élans!
> Tu voles selon. . . .

> Jamais l'espérance,
>     Pas d'orietur.
> Science et patience,
> Le supplice est sûr.

> Plus de lendemain
> Braises de satin
> Votre ardeur
> Est le devoir.

> Elle est retrouvée!
> —Quoi?—l'Éternité.
> C'est la mer mêlée
>     Au soleil.

I became a fabulous opera: I saw that all creatures have a fatality for happiness: action is not life, but a way of spoiling some power, an enervation. Morality is softening of the brain.

Every creature seemed to me to be endowed with several *other* lives. This gentleman does not know what he is doing: he is an angel. This family is a litter of puppies. Before a number of men I would talk aloud with a moment of one of their other existences.—In this way I loved a pig.

Not one of the sophistries of madness,—that madness which one shuts up inside oneself,—have I forgot: I could repeat them all, I remember the system.

My health was endangered. Fear came. I used to fall into periods of sleep lasting for several days, from which I got up again only to resume the most depressing reveries. I was ripe for death, and by a dangerous route my weakness brought me to the confines of Cimmeria, the land of shadow and whirlwinds.

I had to travel, to seek distraction from the spells that were gathered in my head. On the sea which I loved as though it were to wash me clean of defilement, I watched the dawn of the consoling cross. I had been damned by the rainbow. Happiness was my doom, my remorse, my worm: my life must always be too vast to be given up to strength and beauty.

Happiness! Her tooth, sweet unto death, used to warn me at cock-crow,—*ad matutinum,* at the *Christus venit,*—in the gloomiest towns:

> O saisons, ô châteaux!
> Quelle âme est dans défauts!
>
> J'ai fait la magique étude
> Du bonheur, qu'aucun n'élude.
>
> Salut à lui chaque fois
> Que chante le coq gaulois.
>
> Ah! je n'aurai plus d'envie:
> Il s'est chargé de ma vie.
>
> Ce charme a pris âme et corps
> Et dispersé les efforts.
>
> O saisons, ô châteaux!
>
> L'heure de la fuite, hélas!
> Sera l'heure du trépas.
>
> O saisons, ô châteaux!

That is over. To-day I know how to honour beauty.

## THE IMPOSSIBLE

Ah! that life of my childhood, the highroad in all weathers, preternaturally solemn, more disinterested than the best of beggars, proud to have neither country nor friends; what nonsense it was.—And I see it only now,

I was right in despising these good fellows who lose no opportunity for a caress, parasites of the cleanliness and health of our women, nowadays, when they are at such cross purposes with us.

I have been right in all my scorns: because I am running away!

Running away?

I explain.

Only yesterday I was sighing: "Heavens! are there not enough of us damned down here! I myself have been so long already in their company. I know them all. We always recognize one another; we sicken one another. Charity is unknown to us. But we are civil; our relations with society are very respectable." Is it surprising? The world! business men, simple fellows!—We are not looked down on. But the elect, how would they receive us? Now there are surly and joyous persons, not the true elect, since one needs audacity or humility if one is to approach them. They are the only elect. They utter no blessings.

Finding that I have still two pennies of common sense,—that is quickly spent!—I see that my unhappiness comes from not having realized soon enough that we are in the Occident. The Occidental swamps Not that I believe the light altered, form shrunken, movement gone astray. . . . Good! right here my spirit desires absolutely to take upon itself all the cruel developments the spirit has undergone since the end of the Orient. . . . It desires this, does my spirit!

My two pennies of common sense are spent! The spirit is authority. It wants me to be in the Occident. I should have to make it be silent in order to conclude as I should like to.

Crowns of martyrdom, triumphs of art, pride of inventors, ardour of pirates—bade them all go to the devil. I returned to the East and to the ancient and eternal wisdom.—It seems that this is a dream of gross indolence!

Yet, I was not thinking particularly of the pleasure of escaping from modern sufferings. I had not in mind the bastard wisdom of the Koran.—But is it not a real affliction, that ever since that declaration of science, Christianity, man has been *playing,* proving his evidence, satiating himself with the pleasure of repeating those proofs, and living only in that way? Subtle, ridiculous torture; source of my spiritual aberrations. Nature can grow bored, perhaps! M. Prudhomme was born with Christ.

It is not because we cultivate fog? We eat fever with our watery vegetables. And drunkenness! and tobacco! and ignorance! and devotions!—Is all that far enough from the thought of the wisdom of the East, the first country? Why a modern world at all, if such poisons are invented!

The churchmen will say: We understand. But you are talking about the Garden of Eden. Nothing for you in the history of the Oriental peoples.—True; it is of Eden that I was dreaming! What has the purity of ancient races to do with my dreams?

The philosophers: The world has no age. Humanity simply shifts from place to place. You happen to be in the Occident, but you are free to live in your Orient, as old a one as you please,—and to live there comfortably. Don't be a victim. Philosophers, you belong to your Occident.

My spirit, be wary. No violent taking sides to win salvation. Exert yourself!—Ah! science does not move fast enough for us!—But I perceive that my spirit is asleep.

If it were always wide awake from this moment on, we should soon have arrived at the truth, which perhaps surrounds us with its weeping angels! . . . If it had been awake up to now, I should not then have yielded to harmful instincts at an immemorial epoch! . . . If it had always been wide awake, I should be sailing in full wisdom! . . .

O purity! purity!

It is this minute of wakefulness that has given me the vision of purity!—By the spirit one goes to God! Heart-rending misfortune!

## THE LIGHTNING

Human toil! that is the explosion which from time to time lights up my abyss.

"Nothing is vanity; science and forward!" cries the modern Ecclesiastes, which is to say *everybody*. And yet the carcasses of the wicked and of the slothful fall upon the hearts of the rest. . . . Ah! hurry, hurry a little; out there, beyond the night, those rewards, future, everlasting . . . shall we miss them? . . .

What can I do? I know toil of old; and science is too slow. Let prayer gallop and let the light roar. . . . I see perfectly. It is too easy, and the weather is too warm; they get on without me. I have my duty; I will show my pride in it, after the manner of some others, by setting it aside.

My life is worn out. Let us make believe, let us idle away, O pity! And we will live for our own amusement, dreaming monstrous loves, and fantastic universes, complaining and finding fault with the lineaments of the world, acrobat, beggar, artist, bandit,—priest!.On my bed in the hospital, the smell of incense has come back to me so overpoweringly: keeper of the holy perfumes, confessor, martyr. . . .

There I recognize the vile education of my childhood. What then! . . . Go my twenty years if others go twenty. . . .

No! no! at present I rebel against death! Work seems too easy for my pride; my betrayal to the world would be too brief a penalty. At the last moment I should strike out right and left. . . .

Then,—Oh!—dear, poor soul, would eternity not be lost to us!

## MORNING

Had I not *once* an amiable, heroic, fabulous youth, to write on leaves of gold, "too much luck!" Through what crime, through what error, have I earned my present weakness? You who maintain that animals groan with vexation, that sick men despair, that the dead dream ill, try to tell the story of my fall and of my sleep. I myself can no more explain than the beggar with his continual *Paters* and *Ave Marias*. *I no longer know how to talk!*

Yet I believe that to-day I have finished the tale of my hell. It was hell, certainly; the ancient one, whose gates the Son of Man opened.

From the same desert, out of the same night, always my tired eyes woke to the silver star, always, while the Kings of life, the three Magi, heart, soul and mind, did not stir! When shall we go out beyond shores and mountains, to greet the birth of the new toil, of the new wisdom, the flight of tyrants and demons, the end of superstition; to adore,—the first!—Christmas on earth?

The song of the skies, the march of peoples! Slaves, let us not slander life.

## ADIEU

Autumn already!—But why long for a sun that will last forever, when we are busy with the discovery of the divine light,—far from the men who die on the seasons?

Autumn. My bark, whose sails were set in the moveless fog, turns toward the port of misery, the immense city with skies stained by fire and mud. Ah! the rotten rags, the bread soaked with rain, the drunkenness, the thousand loves which crucified me. She will have no end, then, that ghoulish queen of a million souls and bodies, which are dead *and which will be judged!* I see myself again, my skin eaten by mire and plague, my hair, my armpits full of worms, and still bigger worms in my heart, stretched among unknown men, ageless, feelingless . . . I might have died there . . . Frightful evocation! I abhor squalor!

And I am afraid of winter because it is the season of comfort!— Sometimes in the sky I see infinite strands covered with white nations in joy. Above me, a great ship of gold flutters its many-coloured pennons in the morning wind. I have created all pageants, all triumphs, all dramas. I have attempted the invention of new flowers, new stars, new flesh, new tongues. I have believed myself the possessor of supernatural powers. Well! I am going to bury my imagination and my memories! A fine artist's and story-teller's reputation gone to the devil!

I! I who called myself a wizard or an angel, free from every rule of morality, am brought back to earth with a job to look out for and harsh reality to embrace! Peasant!

Am I mistaken? would charity be death's sister to me?

Finally I will ask forgiveness for having fed myself on lies, and I am off.

But not one friendly hand! and where shall I ask for help?

Yes, this new hour is at worst very hard.

For I can say that victory is mine: the teeth-gritting, fire-breathing and pestilential gasps abate. All memories of the world are fading. My last regrets are withdrawn,—envy of beggars, thieves, friends of death, hangers-back of all sorts.—You damned ones, if I were to avenge myself!

It is necessary to be absolutely modern.

No canticles: hold to the step you have gained. Sore night! The dried blood smokes on my face, and I have nothing at my back but this horrible bush! . . . The battle of the spirit is as brutal as the clash of men; but the perception of justice is the pleasure of God alone.

This, however, is the vigil. Welcome every influx of true vigour and tenderness. And at dawn, armed with eager patience, we will enter the splendid towns.

What was I saying about a friendly hand! One advantage is that I can laugh at the old, false passions, and put to shame those lying couples,—I have seen the hell of women down there;—and it will be legitimate for me to *possess the truth m a soul and body.*

April-August, 1873.

## The Drunken Boat

### Translated by Lionel Abel

As I slid down the impassible river narrows,
I felt no longer guided by the bargemen;
From painted stakes they hung, shot through with arrows,
Squalling redskins had taken them for targets.

I did not wait for baggage to embark,
For bearers of British cotton, Flemish stone,
But when my guides lay scalpless in the dark,
The rivers and my will remained, alone.

Muffled as a child in the womb's mesh,
I ran, last winter, in the sea's surf-merriment,
Envy the water's welcome of my flesh,
Peninsulas cracked off by continents!

Kind storms poured out their mischief on my head,
Without the ninny eyes of lantern guides,
Over eternal dungeons of the dead,
Lighter than a cork, I danced the tides.

Tender as flesh of apples to a child,
With stains of blue wine, vomitings, and film,
Up through my shell came the green water wild,
And laved me, splitting grappling hook and helm.

And I have since bathed in the milk and swale
Of the poem sea, infused with stars around,
Devoured its glaucous depths where sometimes floats the pale,
Rapt, brooding body of a man who is drowned.

Where dyeing the deep with deliriums and fires,
And tender rhythms, under day's rutilant roof,
Stronger than whiskey, vaster than your lyres,
Ferments the bitter rust-red froth of love!

I know skies scratched with lightning, waterspouts,
The surf, the current, the evening near to me,
The dawn exalted as a flight of doves,
And I have seen what men believe to see.

I saw the low sun spotted like a snake
Illumine violet curds, and the waves, and the breeze,
Like antique actors with a play to make,
Raise up the trembling blooms of anemones.

I dreamed of dazzling snows upon the laps
Of green nights, and kisses an outcast ocean heard,
The circulation of unforgettable saps,
The blue and yellow cries of phosphorus birds,

For months I followed the hysterical hooves
Of rabid waves in their mad rockward beat,
Nor dreamed the muzzle for those snorting droves
Was lifted by the Virgin's luminous feet.

I touched, do you hear? on Floridas that sang,
Heaped high with flowers and skins of men and eyes
Of panthers, where the burnished rainbows hang
Like reins of green sea sheep, from copper skies.

Fermenting fens, enormous nets, where stirs
Leviathan rotting in a reedy rout;
And waters raving round the calmest waters,
And black gulfs putting the horizons out!

Glaciers, silver suns, pearl waves and enrous skies,
And hideous valleys yellow with disease
Where giant serpents eaten away by flies
Fall with black perfumes from contorted trees!

I would have shown to children these doradoes
Of the blue wave, the golden fish, that sings.
The foam of flowers has blessed my voyaging,
And winds ineffable have lent me wings.

At times a martyr weary of zones and poles,
The sea whose sobbing made my buffets dear,
Showed me shadow flowers in yellow shoals,
Sweeter than a woman, lying near,

Until an island tossed about my side
The quarrels and dung of blond-eyed birds that weep,
And I sailed until across my fragile lines
The bodies of the drowned came down to sleep. . . .

Then I, boat lost beneath the hair of rivers,
Flung by the tempest into birdless ether,
I whom no Monitors, no Hansa schooners
Could have fished up, a carcass drunk with water,

Free, fuming, risen from the purple's heart,
Who bored the sky, a ruddy wall that keeps
For all good poets exquisite jelly tarts,
Moss of the sunlight, dribblings of the deep.

Who running spotted with electric rings,
Black hippocampi answering my cry,
When the blue skies were battered, bleeding things
Under the bludgeonings of red July,

Who trembled hearing fifty leagues away
Behemoth rutting, groan, and Maelstrom's grind,
Eternal spinner of blue peace at play,
I long for Europe, antique, turret-lined.

I saw star-archipelagoes! Islands of delight
Whose delirious skies lie open to the wanderer:
Sleep you self-exiled in unbottomed night,
O countless golden birds, O future Vigor?

But I have wept too much, Dawn breaks the heart, there seems
Vileness in moonlight, in the sun, to me.
Harsh love has stuffed me like a bag with dreams.
Oh! let my keel burst! Let me go to the sea!

I want none of Europe's waters unless it be the pale
Cold murky puddle with the twilight nigh
Where a child may sit with sadness, and let sail
A boat as frail as a May butterfly.

I can no longer, bathing in your swoons,
O waves, raise up their wash to dirty dredgers,
Nor cross the pride of flags, the flame of noons,
Nor swim beneath the horrible eyes of barges!

*Illuminations*

*Translated by Wallace Fowlie*

## AFTER THE FLOOD

As soon as the idea of the Flood had subsided,

A hare stopped in the clover and the swinging flower-bells, and said its prayer through the spider's web to the rainbow.

The precious stones were hiding, and already the flowers were beginning to look up.

The butchers' blocks rose up in the dirty main street, and ships were pulled out toward the sea, piled high as in pictures.

Blood flowed in Blue Beard's house, in the slaughter houses, in the circuses, where the seal of God whitened the windows. Blood and milk flowed.

Beavers set about building. Coffee urns let out smoke in the bars.

In the large house with windows still wet, children in mourning looked at exciting pictures.

A door slammed. On the village square the child swung his arms around, and was understood by the weather vanes and the steeple cocks everywhere, under the pelting rain.

Madame X installed a piano in the Alps. Mass and first Communions were celebrated at the 100,000 altars of the Cathedral.

The caravans departed. And the Hôtel Splendide was built in the chaos of ice and polar night.

Since then, the moon has heard jackals yelping in thyme deserts, and eclogues in wooden shoes growling in the orchard. Finally, in the violet budding grove, Eucharis told me spring was here.

—Gush forth, waters of the pond. Foam, pour over the bridge and over the woods. Black shrouds and organs, lightening and thunder, rise up and spread everywhere. Waters and sorrows, rise up and bring back the floods.

For ever since they have gone—oh! the precious stones buried and the opened flowers!—we have been bored! The Queen, the Witch lighting her coal in the earthen pot, will never tell us what she knows and what we shall never know.

## DAWN

I have held the summer dawn in my arms.

Nothing moved as yet on the fronts of the palaces. The water was dead. Swarms of shadows refused to leave the road to the wood. I walked along, awakening the warm, alive air. Stones looked up, and wings rose up silently.

The first occurrence, in the path already filled with cool white shimmerings, was a flower which told me its name.

I laughed at the blond waterfall which tumbled down through the pine trees. At its silver top I recognized the goddess.

Then I took off her veils one by one. In the path, where I waved my arms. In the field, where I gave away her name to the cock. In the city, she fled between steeples and domes; and running like a thief along the marble wharves, I chased her.

Where the road mounts, near a laurel wood, I wrapped her in all her veils and felt something of the immensity of her body. Dawn and the child collapsed at the edge of the wood.

It was noon when I woke up.

## CHILDHOOD

### I

This idol, black-eyed and yellow-haired, no parents and no palace, but more princely than the Mexican and Flemish fairy story. His land of blatant blue and green, covers beaches named by shipless waves, with names that are ferociously Greek, Slav, Celtic.

At the forest's edge,—the dream flowers tinkle, burst, illuminate,—the girl with the orange lips, her knees crossed in the limpid flood rising up from the fields, a naked body shadowed, penetrated and clothed by rainbows, flowers, the ocean.

Ladies strolling round on the terraces near the sea; giants and children, magnificent blacks in the green-grey moss, jewels erect on the rich ground of groves and thawed gardens,—young mothers and tall sisters whose eyes reflect their pilgrimages, sultanas, princesses of tyrannical walk and costume, foreign girls and some others sweetly unhappy.

The boredom of saying "dear body," "dear heart."

### II

That's she, the little girl behind the rose bushes, and she's dead.—The young mother, also dead, is coming down the steps.—The cousin's carriage crunches the sand.—The small brother (he's in India!) over there in the field of pinks, in front of the sunset.—The old men they've buried upright in the wall covered with gilly-flowers.

A swarm of gold leaves smothers the general's house. They're in the south.—You take the red road to reach the empty inn. The château's up for sale and the shutters are coming loose.—The priest must have taken away the key of the church. Around the park, keepers' cottages are uninhabited. The fences are so high that you can only see the tree tops moving in the wind. Anyway, there's nothing to see there.

The fields roll up to the villages without roosters and without anvils. The sluice is open. Oh! the crosses and the windmills of the desert, the islands and the haystacks!

Magic flowers were buzzing. The slopes rocked him like a cradle. Animals of fabulous beauty walked about. Clouds were massed together over the high seas, made of the warm tears of all time.

### III

In the woods there's a bird whose singing stops you and makes you blush.

There's a clock which doesn't strike.

There's a clay-pit with a nest of white animals.

There's a cathedral coming down and a lake going up.

There's a little carriage abandoned in the woods or rolling down the path, with ribbons all over it.

There's a troupe of child actors, in costumes, whom you can see on the road through the edge of the wood.

And then there's someone who chases you off when you're hungry and thirsty.

### IV

I am the saint in prayer on the terrace like the peaceful animals that graze as far as the sea of Palestine.

I am the scholar in his dark armchair. Branches and rain beat against the library window.

I am the wanderer along the main road running through the dwarfish woods. The noise of the sluices drowns my footsteps. For a long time I can see the sad golden wash of the sunset.

I might be the child abandoned on the wharf setting out for the high seas, or the farm-hand following the path whose top reaches the sky.

The pathways are rough. The slopes are covered with broom. The air is still. How far away are the birds and the springs of water! This must be the end of the world, lying ahead.

### V

Now hire for me the tomb, whitewashed with the lines of cement in bold relief,—far underground.

I lean my elbows on the table, and the lamp lights brightly the newspapers I am fool enough to re-read, and the absurd books.

At a tremendous distance above my subterranean room, houses grow like plants, and fogs gather. The mud is red or black. Monstrous city! Endless night!

Not so high up are the sewers. At my side, nothing but the thickness of the globe. Perhaps there are pits of azure and wells of fire. On those levels perhaps moons and comets, seas and fables meet.

In moments of depression, I imagine sapphire and metal balls. I am master of silence. Why should the appearance of a cellar window turn pale at the corner of the ceiling?

## YOUTH

### 1. SUNDAY

When homework is done, the inevitable descent from heaven and the visitation of memories and the session of rhythms invade the dwelling, the head and the world of the spirit.

—A horse scampers off along the suburban turf and the gardens and the wood lots, besieged by the carbonic plague. Somewhere in the world, a wretched melodramatic woman is sighing for unlikely desertions. Desperadoes are languishing for storms, drunkenness, wounds. Little children are stifling curses along the rivers.

I must study some more to the sound of the consuming work which forms in all the people and rises up in them.

### 2. SONNET

*Man* of usual constitution, wasn't the flesh a fruit hanging in the orchard?—O childhood days!—wasn't the body a treasure to spend?— wasn't love the peril or the strength of Psyche? The earth had slopes fertile in princes and artists, and your descendants and your race drove you to crime and mourning: the world, your fortune and your peril. But now that this work is done, you and your calculations, you and your impatience, are only your dance and your voice, not fixed and not forced, although they are the reason for a double event made up of invention and success, in brotherly and discreet humanity throughout the universe without pictures. Force and right reflect the dance and the voice which are only now appreciated.

### 3. TWENTY YEARS OLD

The exiled voices teach. . . . Physical candour bitterly put in its place. . . . Adagio. Oh! infinite egoism of adolescence, and studious optimism. How full of flowers was the world that summer! Melodies and forms dying. ... A choir, to pacify impotence and absence! A choir of glasses, of night tunes. . . . Yes, and one's nerves go out quickly to hunt.

4

You are still at the stage of the temptation of St. Anthony. The struggle with diminished zeal, grimacings of a child's insolence, collapse and fright. But you will begin this work. All the possibilities of harmony and architecture will rise up around your seat. Perfect and unpredictable beings will offer themselves for your experiments. Around you the curiosity of ancient crowds and idle luxuries will move in dreamily. Your memory and your senses will only serve to feed your creative urge. What will happen to the world when you leave it? Nothing, in any case, will remain of what is now visible.

## WAR

Child, certain skies have sharpened my eyesight. Their characters cast shadows on my face. The Phenomena grew excited.—And now, the everlasting inflexion of moments and the infinity of mathematics hunt me throughout the world where I experience civic popularity and am respected by strange children and overpowering affections.—I dream of a War, of justice or power, of unsuspected logic.

It is as simple as a musical phrase.

## AGONY

Can She have me pardoned for my ambition so everlastingly repressed? Can wealth at the end of my life make up for my years of poverty? Can one day's success make me forget on the shame of my fatal awkwardness?

(Oh! palms and diamonds! Love and power! higher than joy and fame!—at any rate, everywhere, a demon and a god, myself the youth of this being!)

Can accidents of scientific fantasy and organizations of social brotherhood be cherished as the progressive restoration of original innocency? . . .

But the Vampire who makes us behave, stipulates that we play with what she leaves us, or otherwise we'll be queer children.

Let me roll in my wounds, through the heavy air and the sea; in my pains, through the silence of water and the harmful air; in the tortures which jeer at me, through their fiendish and billowy silence.

## DEMOCRACY

"The flag's off to that filthy place, and our speech drowns the sound of the drum.

"In the centres we'll feed the most cynical whoring. We'll smash all logical revolts.

"To the peppery dried up countries!—in the service of the most gigantic industrial or military exploitation.

"Goodbye to this place. No matter where we're off to. We conscripts of good will are going to display a savage philosophy: ignorant in science, rakes where our comfort is concerned; and let the world blow up! This is the real march. Forward, men!"

## H

All forms of monstrosity violate the atrocious gestures of Hortense. Her solitude is erotic mechanics; her weariness is the dynamics of love. Under the guardianship of childhood, she has been, at many periods of time, the passionate hygiene of races. Her door is opened to poverty. There the morals of real beings disembody in her passion or her action. O terrible thrill of new loves on the blood covered ground and in the white air! Find Hortense.

## STORY

A Prince was tired of merely spending his time perfecting conventionally generous impulses. He could foretell amazing revolutions of love, and suspected his wives of being able to give him more than their complacency, enhanced with ideals and wealth. He wanted to see truth and the time of full desire and satisfaction. He wanted this, even if it was a misuse of piety. At least he possessed a large reserve of human power.

All the wives who had known him were murdered. What slaughter in the garden of beauty! They blessed him when the sword came down. He did not order any new wives. The wives reappeared.

He killed the men who followed him, after hunting or drinking with them. They all followed him.

He took delight in cutting the throats of the pet animals. He set fire to the palaces. He fell on the servants and hacked them to pieces.—The servants, the gold roofs, the splendid animals were still there.

Can man reach ecstasy in destruction and be rejuvenated by cruelty? His people made no complaint and no one offered him any advice.

One evening when he was proudly riding his horse, a Genie

appeared, of unspeakable, unmentionable beauty. His face and his bearing gave promise of a rich complex love, of an indescribable unbearable happiness. The Prince and the Genie killed one another probably in the prime of life. How could they have failed to die of it? Together, therefore, they died.

But this prince passed away, in his palace, at a normal age. The Prince was Genie. The Genie was Prince.

Our desires are deprived of cunning music.

## CIRCUS

Husky fellows. Some of them have exploited your worlds. Without cares and in no hurry to use their brilliant faculties and their knowledge of your consciences. What virile men! Eyes deadened, like a summer's night, red and black, tri-coloured, of steel spotted with golden stars; faces deformed, ashen, pale, ruddy; wild hoarseness! The cruel demeanour of decorations!—There are some young fellows—what would they think of Fauntleroy?—with dangerous voices and terrifying resources. They are sent to the city to put on airs, decked out in disgusting finery.

Oh! the most violent Paradise of the enraged smile! No comparison with your Fakirs and other stage antics. In improvised, costumes and in the style of a bad dream, they recite sad poems and perform tragedies of brigands and spiritual demi-gods such as history or religion never had. Popular and maternal scenes are mixed with bestial poses and love by Chinese, Hottentots, gipsies, fools, hyenas, Molochs, old fits of madness and wily demons. They would interpret new plays and sentimental songs. As master jugglers they transform the place and the characters and use magnetic comedy. Their eyes catch fire, their blood sings, their bones grow big, tears and red rivulets stream. Their farce or their terror lasts a minute or for months on end.

I alone have the key of this wild circus.

## ANCIENT

Graceful son of Pan! Under your brow crowned with flowers and berries, your eyes, precious balls, move. Spotted with dark streaks, your cheeks look hollow. Your fangs glisten. Your chest is like a lyre and tinklings move up and down your white arms. Your heart beats in that abdomen where your double sex sleeps. Walk at night and move gently this thigh, then this other thigh and this left leg.

## BOTTOM

Reality being too prickly for my lofty character, I became at my lady's a big blue-grey bird flying up near the mouldings of the ceiling and dragging my wings after me in the shadows of the evening.

At the foot of the baldaquino supporting her precious jewels and her physical masterpieces, I was a fat bear with purple gums and thick sorry-looking fur, my eyes of crystal and silver from the consoles.

Everything grew dark like a burning aquarium. In the morning—a battling June dawn—I ran to the fields, an ass, trumpeting and brandishing my grievance, until the Sabines came from the suburbs to hurl themselves on my chest.

## BEING BEAUTEOUS

Standing tall before snow, a being of beauty. Death whistles and rings of muffled music cause this worshipped body to rise up, expand and tremble like a ghost. Scarlet and black wounds break out on the proud flesh. The very colours of life deepen, dance and stand out from the vision, in the yard. Tremblings rise and threaten, and the persistent taste of these effects combining with the whistle of men and the discordant music which the world, far behind us, throws to our mother of beauty. She draws back and stands up. Our bones are reclothed with a new amorous body.

Oh! the ashen face, the horsehair emblem, the crystal arms! The canon on which I must fall, in the medley of trees and light air!

## SCENES

Ancient Comedy continues its harmonies and divides up its idylls: Streets of stages.

A long wooden pier stretching from one end of a rocky field to the other, where the wild crowd wanders under the bare trees.

In corridors of black gauze, following the steps of passers-by under the lanterns and leaves.

Bird actors from mystery plays come down on to the stonework of the pontoon bridge which is moved up and down by the protected line of spectators' boats.

Lyric scenes, accompanied by flute and drum, bow gracefully in corners, under the ceilings round modern club rooms or ancient Oriental halls.

The fairy-play takes place at the top of an amphitheatre crowned with foliage—or is performed in a modulated key for Bœotians, in the darkness of moving trees or the crest of fields.

The opéra-comique is divided on our stage at the line of intersection of ten partitions placed between the gallery and the footlights.

## LIVES

### I

Oh! the huge avenues of the Holy Land and the terraces of the temple! What has happened to the Brahmin who taught me the Proverbs? From then and from there I can still see even the old women! I remember silvery hours and sun near rivers, the hand of the country on my shoulder, and our caresses, as we stood in the fiery fields.—A flight of red pigeons thunders around my thoughts.—In exile here, I had a stage on which to perform the dramatic masterpieces of all literatures. I might tell you about unheard of wealth. I follow the story of the treasures you found. I see the next chapter! My wisdom is as neglected as chaos is. What is my void compared with the stupefaction awaiting you?

### II

I am a far more deserving inventor than all those who went before me; a musician, in fact, who found something resembling the key of love. At present, a noble from a meagre countryside with a dark sky. I try to feel emotion over the memory of a mendicant childhood, over my apprenticeship when I arrived wearing wooden shoes, polemics, five or six widowings, and a few wild escapades when my strong head kept me from rising to the same pitch as my comrades. I don't miss what I once possessed of divine happiness: the calm of this despondent countryside gives a new vigour to my terrible scepticism. But since this scepticism can no longer be put into effect, and since I am now given over to a new worry—I expect to become a very wicked fool.

### III

In an attic where at the age of twelve I was locked up, I knew the world and illustrated the human comedy. In a wine cellar I learned history. At some night celebration, in a Northern city, I met all the wives of former painters. In an old back street in Paris I was taught the classical sciences. In a magnificent palace, surrounded by all the Orient, I finished my long work and spent my celebrated retirement. I have invigorated my blood. I am released from my duty. I mustn't even think of that any longer. I am really beyond the tomb, and without work.

## PHRASES

When the world is reduced to a single dark wood for our two pairs of dazzled eyes,—to a beach for two faithful children,—to a musical house for our clear understanding,—then I shall find you.

When there is only one old man on earth, lonely, peaceful, handsome, living in unsurpassed luxury, then I am at your feet.

When I have realized all your memories, when I am the girl who can tie your hands,—then I will stifle you.

*     *     *

When we are very strong, who draws back? or very happy, who collapses from ridicule? When we are very bad, what can they do to us?

Dress up, dance, laugh. I will never be able to throw Love out of the window.

*     *     *

Comrade of mine, beggar girl, monstrous child! How little you care about the wretched women, and the machinations and my embarrassment. Join us with your impossible voice, oh your voice! the one flatterer of this base despair.

A dark morning in July. The taste of ashes in the air, the smell of wood sweating in the hearth, steeped flowers, the devastation of paths, drizzle over the canals in the fields, why not already playthings and incense?

*     *     *

I stretched out ropes from spire to spire; garlands from window to window; golden chains from star to star, and I dance.

*     *     *

The high pond is constantly steaming. What witch will rise up against the white sunset? What purple flowers are going to descend?

*     *     *

While public funds disappear in brotherly celebrations, a bell of pink fire rings in the clouds.

*     *     *

Arousing a pleasant taste of Chinese ink, a black powder gently rains on my night. I lower the jets of the chandelier, throw myself on to the bed, and, turning toward the dark, I see you, O my daughters and queens!

## MORNING OF DRUNKENNESS

*My* story of the Good and the Beautiful! Terrible fanfare of music where I never lose step! Magical rack! Hurrah for the miraculous work and for the marvellous body, for the first time! It all began with the laughter of children, and will end there. This poison will still be in my veins even when the fanfare dies away and I return to the earlier discord. And now that I am so worthy of this torture, let me fervently gather in the superhuman promise made to my created body and soul. This promise, this madness! Elegance, science, violence! They promised me they would bury in the darkness the tree of good and evil, and deport tyrannical codes of honesty so that I may bring forward my very pure love. It all began with feelings of disgust and it ended—since I couldn't seize its eternity on the spot,—it ended with a riot of perfumes.

Laughter of children, discreetness of slaves, coldness of virgins, horror of figures and objects from here, be consecrated by the memory of that night. It began in slyness and it came to an end with angels of fire and ice.

Brief night of intoxication, holy night! even if it was only for the mask you bequeathed to me. I assert you, method! I am not forgetting that yesterday you glorified each of our ages. I believe in that poison. I can give all of my existence each day.

Behold the age of Murderers.

## VAGABONDS

Poor brother! What terrible nights I owed him! "I had no deep feeling for the affair. I played on his weakness. Through my fault, we would return to exile and slavery." He believed I had a very queer form of bad luck and innocence, and he added upsetting reasons.

With a jeer I answered my Satanic doctor, and left by the window. Along the countryside, streaked with bands of rare music, I created phantoms of a future night parade.

After that vaguely hygienic distraction, I lay down on straw. And almost every night, as soon as I was asleep, my poor brother would get up, his mouth dry and his eyes protruding—just as he dreamed himself to be—and would drag me into the room yelling his dream of a sad fool.

In deepest sincerity, I had pledged to convert him back into his primitive state of a Sun-god,—and we wandered, sustained by wine from caverns and traveller's crust, with me impatient to find the place and the formula.

## DAILY NOCTURNE

A gust of wind makes operadic cracks in the partitions, confuses the pivoting of worm eaten roofs, blows away the walls of hearths, blots out the windows. Leaning with one foot on a gargoyle, I came down past the vineyards in a coach whose period is clear enough in its convex mirrors, its swelling panels and its round sofas. Hearse of my sleep, all alone, shepherd's hut of my tomfoolery, the carriage turns on the grass of the fading highway: and in a blemish at the top of the right hand glass white lunar figures, leaves and breasts revolve.—A very deep green and blue invade the picture. We can unharness near a patch of gravel.

—Here we can whistle for the storm, and Sodoms and Solymas, and wild beasts and armies,

—(Will the poste-chaise and dream animals take over in the most stifling groves to push me down to the level of my eyes in the silk water?)

—And send us, whipped by the thumping waters and the spilled drinks, to roll over the barking of the bulldogs. . . .

—A gust of wind blows away the walls of the hearth.

## FLOWERS

From a gold terrace,—amidst silken cords, grey veils, green velvets and crystal discs which darken as bronze in the sun,—I see the foxglove opening on a tapestry of silver threads, eyes and hair.

Pieces of yellow gold sown on the agate, mahogany pillars supporting an emerald dome, bouquets of white satin and delicate stalks of rubies surround the water rose.

Like a god with large blue eyes and a snow body, the sea and the sky entice to the marble stairs the swarm of young strong roses.

## SEAPIECE

Chariots of silver and copper—
Bows of steel and silver—
Beat the foam,—
Raise up the stumps of bramble.
The currents of the moor
And the huge ruts of the ebb tide,
Flow circularly toward the east,
Toward the pillars of the forest,
Toward the poles of the pier,
Whose angle is struck by whirls of light.

## WINTER PARTY

The waterfall resounds behind the *opéra-comique* cabins. Candelabra continue, in the neighbouring orchards and paths of the labyrinth, the greens and reds of the sunset. Nymphs of Horace with First Empire head-dress,—Siberian dances, Chinese women by Boucher.

## FAIRY WORLD

For Helen the decorative sap conspired in the virginal darkness and the impassive light in the skiey silence. The heat of summer was entrusted to silent birds and the appropriate languor to a priceless mourning barge moving through waters of dead loves and collapsed perfumes.

After the time when the wives of the woodcutters sang to the sound of the cascade in the ruins of the forest, after the bells of the animals sounded to the echo of the valleys and the cries of the steppes.—

For Helen's childhood the furs and the shadows trembled, and the breasts of the poor and the legends of heaven.

And her eyes and her dancing still superior to the shafts of precious light, to waves of cold, to the pleasure of the unique setting and the unique moment.

## WORKERS

That warm February morning. The unseasonable south came to stimulate our memories of ridiculous poverty, all our youthful want.

Henrika had on a skirt of brown and white checkered cotton which must have been worn a hundred years ago, a bonnet with ribbons and a silk scarf. It was sadder than mourning. We took a walk in the suburbs. The sky was grey, and that wind from the south brought out all the bad smells from the ruined gardens and the dried up meadows.

This didn't tire my wife as much as myself. In a pool left by the flood of the month before, on quite a high path, she showed me some very small fish.

The city, with its smoke and noise from the looms, followed us as far as we walked. Oh! that other world, that dwelling blessed by heaven, and the cool shade! The south reminded me of the wretched events of my childhood, of my torments in summer time, of the horrible amount of strength and science which fate has always taken away from me. No! We will not spend the summer in this miserly place where we will never be anything but betrothed orphans. I don't want these strong arms to drag any longer *a beloved image.*

## BRIDGES

Grey crystal skies. A strange pattern of bridges, some straight, some arched, others going down at oblique angles to the first, and these shapes repeating themselves in other lighted circuits of the canal, but all of them so long and light that the banks, heavy with domes, are lowered and shrunken. Some of these bridges are still covered with hovels. Others support masts, signals, thin parapets. Minor chords cross one another and diminish, ropes come up from the shores. You can see a red jacket and perhaps other costumes and musical instruments. Are they popular tunes, bits of castle concerts, remnants of public hymns? The water is grey and blue, as wide as an arm of the sea.—A white ray, falling from the top of the sky, blots out this comedy.

## CITY

I am an ephemeral and a not-too-discontented citizen of a metropolis obviously modern because every known taste has been avoided in the furnishings and in the outsides of the houses as well as in the lay-out of the city. Here you would not discover the least sign of any monument of superstition. In short, morals and speech are reduced to their simplest expression. These millions of people who have no need of knowing one another conduct their education, their trade and their old age, with such similarity that the duration of their lives must be several times less long than, according to some insane statistics, is the case with the people on the continent. From my window, I see new ghosts rolling through thick everlasting coal smoke—our shadow in the woods, our summer night—new Eumenides in front of my cottage which is my country and my heart since everything here resembles it—Death without tears, our active daughter and servant, a desperate Love, and a pretty Crime crying in the mud of the street.

## RUTS

In the right hand corner of the park the summer dawn stirs up leaves and mists and noises, and the mounds on the left hand side hold in their purple shade the countless swift ruts of the wet road. Fairy procession.' Yes, wagons loaded with animals of gilded wood, poles and gaily-striped cloth, to the gallop of twenty spotted circus horses, and children and men on their most amazing beasts;—twenty vehicles embossed, with flags and flowers like ancient or story-book carriages, full of children all dressed for an outing in the suburbs.—Coffins, too, under their dark canopy with their pitch-black plumes, rolling along to the trot of large blue and black mares.

## CITIES I

They are cities! They are a people for whom these Alleghanies and dream Lebanons have risen up. Swiss chalets of crystal and wood move along invisible rails and pulleys. Old craters girdled by colossi and copper palm trees roar tunefully in the midst of fires. The sounds of love feasts ring out over the canals suspended behind the chalets. The pack of chimes clamours in the gorges. Gilds of gigantic singers come together in clothes and banners as shining as the light on mountain tops. On platforms, within precipices, Rolands blare forth their valour. On foot bridges spanning the abyss and the roofs of inns, the burning sky decks out masts. The collapse of apotheoses joins the fields with the highlands where seraphic centauresses move about in avalanches. Above the level of the highest crests, a sea, disturbed by the eternal birth of Venus, heavy with Orphic navies and the roar of pearls and precious shells, the sea sometimes grows dark with mortal splendour. On the slopes, harvests of flowers as big as our arms and our tankards bellow. Long lines of Mabs in red and opal dresses come up from the valleys. There, with their feet in the waterfall and the briars, deer suckle at the breasts of Diana. The Bacchantes of the suburbs sob and the moor burns and shouts. Venus goes into the caverns of blacksmiths and hermits. Groups of belfries intone the ideas of the people. Unfamiliar music comes from castles built of bones. All legends gyrate and the impulses of the living hurl themselves about in the villages. The paradise of storms comes to its end. The savages dance ceaselessly in the celebration of night. And for one hour, I went down into the animated Bagdad boulevard where groups sang of the joy of new work, in a sluggish breeze, moving about without eluding the fabulous phantoms of mountains where people had to find themselves again.

What good arms, what precious hour will give me back that place from where come my sleep and my slightest movements?

## CITIES II

The official acropolis surpasses the most colossal conceptions of modern barbarism. Impossible to express the flat daylight produced by this unchanging grey sky, the imperial glitter of the buildings and the eternal snow on the ground. In a singular taste for the gigantic they reproduced all the classical architectural marvels, and I visit exhibitions of paintings in rooms twenty times larger than Hampton Court. What paintings! A Norwegian Nebuchadnezzar built the stairways of the government buildings; the underlings I saw are already prouder than . . ., and I trembled at the sight of the guards of the colossi and the building officials. By arranging the buildings into squares, closed courtyards and terraces, they cheated the cab-drivers. The parks represent a primitive nature artfully and proudly laid out. The upper part of the city has inexplicable parts: a river from the sea, without boats, unfolds its blue slate water between wharves supporting tremendous candelabra. A short bridge leads to a postern right under the dome of the Sainte-Chapelle. This dome is an artistic framework of steel, about 15,000 feet in diameter.

From a few points of the copper foot-bridges, and platforms and stairways surrounding the markets and pillars, I thought I could estimate the depth of the city! This is the miracle I wasn't able to judge: what are the levels of the other parts above or below the acropolis? For the foreigner of our day, reconnoitring is impossible. The business quarter is a circus constructed in a uniform style, with arcade galleries. You can't see any shops, but the snow on the highway is flattened; a few nabobs, as rare as Sunday morning walkers in London, are moving toward a diamond coach. A few divans of red velvet. They serve North Pole drinks at a price between 800 and 8,000 rupees. While on the point of looking for theatres in this circus, I tell myself that the shops must contain fairly tragic dramas. I think there are policemen. But the law must be so unusual that I give up imagining what adventurers are like here.

The suburb, as elegant as a beautiful street in Paris, enjoys an air of light, and the democratic constituency numbers a few hundred souls. There too, the houses don't follow one another. The suburb melts strangely into the country, the "county" filling the eternal west with forests and gigantic plantations, where savage nobles hunt their news columns in the fight which they invented.

## METROPOLITAN

From the blue straits to Ossian's sea, over the rose-orange sand washed by a wine-coloured sky, crystal boulevards have risen up and crossed, immediately settled by poor young families who get their food at the fruit dealers. Nothing rich.—Just the city.

From the asphalt desert flee in a straight line helmets, wheels, barges, rumps,—in confusion with the sheets of fog spaced in horrible bands in the sky which bends back, withdraws and comes down, formed by the most treacherous black smoke which the Ocean in mourning can make.—Just the battle.

Look up: this wood bridge, arched; these last vegetable gardens of Samaria; these illuminated masks under the lantern whipped by the cold night; the silly water nymph in her noisy dress, in the lower part of the river; these luminous skulls in the pea rows,—and other bewitchments.—Just the country.

These roads lined with fences and walls, their gardens bursting over them and the terrible flowers called hearts and sisters, damask cursing languorously,—possessions of fairy-like aristocracies ultra-Rhenish, Japanese, Guaranian, still capable of receiving the music of the ancients,—and there are inns which will never open again now,—there are princesses, and if you are not too overwrought, the study of the stars—just the sky.

In the morning when with Her, you fought in those shimmerings of snow, the green lips, the ice, the black flags and blue rays, and the red perfumes of the polar sun.—Just your strength.

## BARBARIAN

Long after the days and the seasons, the men and the countries,

The flag of red meat over the silk of the seas and the Arctic flowers (but they don't exist).

Recovering from the old blasts of heroism—which still attack our heart and our head—far from the former assassins,

Oh! the flag of red meat over the silk of the seas and the Arctic flowers (but they don't exist)—

Happiness!

The blazing fires, streaming in the frosty gusts.—Happiness! The fire's in the rain of the wind of diamonds hurled down by the world's heart endlessly burned for us. O world!

(Far from the old places and the old fire we hear and smell.)

Fires and foam. Music, turning of the abysses and collisions of icicles with the stars.

O happiness, O world, O music! There, forms, sweating, hair and eyes, floating. And white tears, boiling—O happiness!—and the voice of a woman coming from the depths of the volcanoes and arctic grottoes.

The flag. . . .

## PROMONTORY

The golden dawn and the tremulous evening find our brig out at sea, opposite this villa and its dependencies, which form a promontory as extensive as Epirus and the Peloponnesus, or as the large island of Japan, or Arabia! Temples lighted up by the return of theories, tremendous views of modern coastal defences; dunes illuminated by warm flowers and bacchanalia; great canals of Carthage and Embankments of a degenerate Venice; mild erupting Etnas and crevasses of flowers and glacier waters; outside laundries surrounded by German poplars; mounds in odd parks where the top of a Japanese tree bends down; and circular façades of "Royals" or "Grands" of Scarborough and Brooklyn; and their railways flank, hollow out and dominate the outlay of this Hotel, which has been picked from the history of the most ornate and the biggest buildings of Italy, America and Asia, whose windows and terraces, now full of lighting appliances, drinks and redolent breezes, are opened to the spirit of the travellers and nobles—who allow by day all the tarantellas of the coast and even the ritournellas of the illustrious valleys of art, to decorate in a miraculous way the façades of the Palace. Promontory.

## DEPARTURE

Seen enough. The vision met itself in every kind of air.

Had enough. Noises of cities in the evening, in the sunlight, and forever.

Known enough. The haltings of life. Oh! Noises and Visions!

Departure in new affection and sound.

## ROYALTY

One fine morning, in a land of very gentle people, a handsome man and woman cried out in the public square. "My friends, I want her to be queen." "I want to be queen." She laughed and trembled. He spoke to his friends of a revelation, of a trial ended. They swooned over each other.

They actually were monarchs for an entire morning, when crimson draperies were hung over the houses, and for the entire afternoon when they walked toward the palm gardens.

## TO REASON

A tap with your finger on the drum releases all sounds and begins the new harmony.

One step of yours, and the new men rise up and march.

Your head turns aside: new love! Your head turns back: new love!

The children sing to you: "Change our fate, overcome the plague and begin with time." They beg you, "Raise where you wish the substance of our fortune and our prayers."

You will go everywhere, since you have come from all time.

## MYSTIC

On the slope of the hill, the angels whirl their woollen robes in the steel and emerald grasses.

Meadows of flame leap up to the top of the rise. On the left, the earth of the crest has been trampled on by all the murderers and battles, and all the sounds of disaster flash in their orbit. Behind the crest on the right, the line of the east and progress.

And while the band, at the top of the picture, is formed by the whirling and leaping noise of conch shells and nights of men,

The flowering beauty of the stars and of the sky and of all else comes down opposite the hill, like a basket, close to our face, and makes the hollow below sweet smelling and blue.

## VIGILS

### I

It is enlightened rest, no fever no languor, on the bed or on the grass.

It is the friend, who is neither strong nor weak. The friend.

It is the beloved, not tormenting not tormented. The beloved.

The air and the world not sought after. Life.

—Was it this then?

—And the dream brought coolness.

### II

The lighting comes back to the beam. From the two far sides of the room, commonplace settings, harmonic elevations merge. The wall opposite the guard is a psychological series of sections of friezes, atmospheric bands and geological occurrences.—An intense swift dream of sentimental groups with men of all characters in the midst of all appearances.

### III

The lamps and the rugs of the vigil make the sound of waves at night along the keel and around the steerage deck.

The sea of the vigil, like the breasts of Amelia.

The tapestries, half-way up, the lace undergrowth, emerald-coloured, where the doves of the vigil fly.

*    *    *

The plaque of the black hearth, real suns of the shores: ah! well of magic; this time, a solitary vision of dawn.

## HISTORIC EVENING

For example, on some evening when the innocent tourist has retired from our economic turmoil, the hands of the master bring to life the harpsichord of the fields. They play cards at the bottom of the lake, a mirror reflecting queens and favourites. They have saints, veils, weavings of harmony and chromatic legends in the sunset.

He shudders at the passing of hunts and hordes. Comedy trickles on to the lawn platforms. And the embarrassment of the poor and the feeble on these stupid floor plans!

Before his slavish vision, Germany builds itself up toward the moons; Tartar deserts are lighted up; ancient revolutions rumble in the centre of the Celestial Empire; over the rock stairways and armchairs a small white flat world, Africa and the Wests, is going to be erected. Then a ballet of well-known seas and nights, a valueless chemistry, and impossible melodies.

The same middle-class magic wherever the mail train puts us down! The most elementary physicist feels it is no longer possible to undergo this personal atmosphere, a fog of physical remorse, whose very existence is already a trial.

No! The moment of the cauldron, of seas swept away, of underground conflagrations, of the planet carried off, of resulting exterminations, certainties indicated with so little maliciousness in the Bible and in the Norns which it will be the duty of a serious man to watch.—Yet it will not give the impression of a legend!

## MOTION

The swaying motion on the bank of the river falls,
The chasm at the stern-post,
The swiftness of the hand-rail,
The huge passing of the current
Conduct by unimaginable lights
And chemical newness
Voyagers surrounded by the water spouts of the valley
And the current.

They are the conquerors of the world
Seeking a personal chemical fortune;
Sports and comfort travel with them;
They take the education
Of races, classes and animals, on this boat
Repose and dizziness
To the torrential light
To the terrible nights of study.
For from the talk among the apparatus, blood, flowers, fire, jewels,
From the agitated accounts on this fleeing deck,
—You can see, rolling like a dyke beyond the hydraulic motor road,
Monstrous, illuminated endlessly,—their stock of studies;
They, chased into harmonic ecstasy,
And the heroism of discovery.

In the most startling atmospheric happenings,
A youthful couple withdraws into the archway,
—Is it an ancient coyness that can be forgiven?—
And sings and stands guard.

## DEVOTIONS

To Sister Louise Vanaen de Voringhem: with her blue coif turned toward the North Sea. Pray for the shipwrecked.

To Sister Léonie Aubois d'Ashby. Baou—the buzzing smelly summer grass.—Pray for the fever of mothers and children.

To Lulu—a devil—who has kept a taste for oratories of the time of friends and her incomplete education. Pray for men!—To Madame . . .

To the adolescent I once was. To that holy elder, hermitage or mission.

To the spirit of the poor. And to a very high ranking clergy.

As well as to every devotion in every place of age-old worship and to such events where one has to go, to observe the aspirations of the moment or our own ingrained vice.

This evening to Circeto of the cold heights, fat as a fish, and illuminated like the ten months of the red night,—(her heart amber and spirited),—for my one prayer silent as those night regions and preceding bravery more violent than this polar chaos.

At all costs and in every manner, even in metaphysical journeys.—But no more *thens*.

## SALE

For sale what the Jews haven't sold, what nobility and crime haven't enjoyed, what the fatal love and the infernal honesty of the masses do not know; what time and science need not recognize;

Revived Voices; the brotherly awakening of all choral and orchestral power and their immediate application; the unique opportunity of freeing our senses!

For sale priceless Bodies, not belonging to any known race, world, sex, progeny! Wealth rising up at each step! Sale of diamonds with no control!

For sale anarchy for the masses; irrepressible satisfaction for superior amateurs; terrible death for the faithful and lovers!

For sale dwellings and migrations, sports, fantasies and perfect comfort, with the noise, movement and future they create!

For sale results of mathematics and unheard of scales of harmony. Discoveries and unsuspected terminologies, immediate possession,

Wild and infinite leap to invisible splendour, to immaterial delights,—and its ravishing secrets for each vice—and its terrifying gaiety for the masses.

For sale Bodies, voices, the tremendous unquestionable wealth, what will never be sold. The salesmen have not reached the end of the sale! Travellers don't have to render accounts immediately!

### GENIE

He is affection and the present moment because he has thrown open the house to the snow foam of winter and to the noises of summer, he who purified drinking water and food, who is the enchantment of fleeing places and the superhuman delight of resting places. He is affection and future, the strength and love which we, erect in rage and boredom, see pass by in the sky of storms and the flags of ecstasy.

He is love, perfect and reinvented measure, miraculous, unforeseen reason, and eternity: machine loved for its qualities of fate. We have all known the terror of his concession and ours: delight in our health, power of our faculties, selfish affection and passion for him,—who loves us because his life is infinity. . . .

And we recall him and he sets forth. . . . And if Adoration moves and rings, his promise rings: "Down with these superstitions, these other bodies, these couples and ages. This is the time which has gone under!"

He will not go away, he will not come down again from some heaven, he will not redeem the anger of women, the laughter of men, or all that Sin: for it's done now, since he is and since he is loved.

His breathing, his heads, his racings: the terrifying swiftness of form and action when they are perfect.

Fertility of the mind and vastness of the world!

His body! the dreamed of liberation, the collapse of grace joined with new violence! all that he sees! all the ancient kneelings and the penalties cancelled as he passes by.

His day! the abolition of all noisy and restless suffering within more intense music.

His step! Migrations more tremendous than early invasions.

He and I! pride more benevolent than lost charity.

O world! and the limpid song of new woe!

He knew us all and loved us. May we, this winter night, from cape to cape, from the noisy pole to the castle, from the crowd to the beach, from vision to vision, our strength and our feelings tired, hail him and see him and send him away, and under tides and on the summit of snow deserts follow his eyes, his breathing, his body, his day.

### THE END

Printed in the USA
CPSIA information can be obtained
at www.ICGtesting.com
LVHW040518270923
759186LV00015B/629